The Countries

Iceland

Kristin Van Cleaf
ABDO Publishing Company

Published by ABDO Publishing Company, 8000 West 78th Street, Edina, Minnesota 55439.
Copyright © 2008 by Abdo Consulting Group, Inc. International copyrights reserved in all
countries. No part of this book may be reproduced in any form without written permission from the
publisher. The Checkerboard Library™ is a trademark and logo of ABDO Publishing Company.

Printed in the United States.

Interior Photos: Alamy pp. 4, 6, 9, 19, 21, 22, 25, 27, 31, 33, 37; Corbis pp. 5, 11, 13, 29, 35;
    Getty Images pp. 18, 20, 36

Editors: Heidi M.D. Elston, BreAnn Rumsch
Art Direction & Maps: Neil Klinepier

Library of Congress Cataloging-in-Publication Data

Van Cleaf, Kristin, 1976-
 Iceland / Kristin Van Cleaf.
     p. cm. -- (The countries)
 Includes index.
 ISBN 978-1-59928-784-3
 1. Iceland--Juvenile literature. I. Title.

DL305.V36 2008
949.12--dc22

                           2007010181

Contents

Halló!

Hello from Iceland! This country is an island in the North Atlantic Ocean. Even so, it is considered part of Europe. But unlike most European countries, people did not **inhabit** Iceland until the AD 700s.

Iceland is a land of natural wonders. These include volcanoes, earthquakes, hot springs, geysers, glaciers, and lava beds. In fact, about one-tenth of Iceland's land is made of glacier ice and cooled lava.

The Strokkur geyser shoots water every three to seven minutes!

Iceland's location in the Atlantic Ocean affects more than the makeup of the land. It also determines the climate. Iceland's nearness to the **Arctic Circle** means the country is dark during most of the winter. But in the summer, the sun shines nearly the whole day!

Halló *from Iceland!*

Throughout history, Icelanders have struggled against foreign control and natural disasters. But, they have remained strong. Today, Icelanders work to preserve their language and **culture** from foreign influence. Many people still produce native crafts, such as knitted goods. Iceland is a modern nation. It is not crowded. And, the people enjoy a high standard of living.

Fast Facts

OFFICIAL NAME: Republic of Iceland
CAPITAL: Reykjavík

LAND
- Area: 39,769 square miles (103,001 sq km)
- Highest Point: Hvannadalshnúkur at 6,952 feet (2,119 m)

PEOPLE
- Population: 299,388
- Major Cities: Reykjavík, Kópavogur, Hafnarfjördhur, Akureyri
- Official Language: Icelandic
- Religions: Lutheranism, Roman Catholicism, other Christian

GOVERNMENT
- Form: Parliamentary democracy
- Head of State: President
- Head of Government: Prime minister
- Legislature: Unicameral parliament
- Nationhood: June 17, 1944

ECONOMY
- Agricultural Products: Potatoes, green vegetables, mutton, dairy products, fish
- Mining Products: Diatomite
- Manufactured Products: Fish processing equipment, aluminum, ferrosilicon, diatomite
- Money: Icelandic krona (1 krona = 100 aurar)

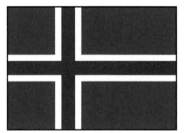

Iceland's flag

Icelandic kronur

Timeline

AD 700s	Iceland is inhabited for the first time
874	Ingólfr Arnarson and Hallveig Fródadóttir settle in Iceland; Reykjavík is founded
930	The people of Iceland create the world's first parliament, the Althing
1100s & 1200s	Iceland's great works of literature are written down for the first time
1262 to 1264	The Althing signs a treaty making Norway's king the ruler of Iceland
1380	Norway and Denmark unite; Denmark assumes control of Iceland
1918	The Treaty of Union makes Iceland an independent state under the Danish monarchy
1944	The Treaty of Union ends; on June 17, the Republic of Iceland is created; Iceland's current constitution is written.
1946	Iceland joins the United Nations
1949	Iceland becomes a member of NATO

Not-So-Ancient History

Iceland's history is as **unique** as its land and climate. The first people to **inhabit** Iceland were probably a few Irish hermits. They are believed to have briefly lived there in the AD 700s. They called the island Thule. Some stories say that Irish monks lived there for a time as well.

Most historians believe that the first permanent settler was a Viking named Ingólfr Arnarson. Ingólfr and his wife, Hallveig Fródadóttir, moved to Iceland from Norway in 874. They built a homestead at a site Ingólfr named Reykjavík (RAY-kyah-veek).

During the next 60 years, more Vikings and Norsemen settled in Iceland. The Norse people worshipped gods such as Odin and Thor. Chiefs called *godar* organized these religious beliefs. The *godar* were considered the ruling class in Iceland.

By the end of this settlement period, the country was in need of organized leadership. So in 930, the people created an assembly called the Althing at Thingvellir (THEENG-gveh-lihr). At the same time, the people created a code of laws. However, there was still no head of state.

In the 900s, Norway's king sent **missionaries** to Iceland to spread Christianity. As a result, in about 999 the Althing decided Icelanders would become Christians. The change was peaceful.

The country flourished in these years. The people hunted, raised livestock, and fished. They created a large **fleet**. And Icelanders traded various goods such as cloth, wool, and hides with other Europeans.

The 1100s and 1200s are known as the golden age of literature in Iceland. Poets and tellers of **sagas** became well known. And for the first time, much of the people's literature was written down.

However, this golden era didn't last. **Economic** and social troubles soon began.

An early Icelandic farm consisted of a group of buildings made of turf and stone. Turf was used in place of wood, because Iceland did not have any large trees.

In the early 1200s, **civil wars** broke out. At the same time, King Haakon IV of Norway was trying to take control of Iceland.

King Haakon took advantage of the fighting to influence Iceland's leaders. From 1262 to 1264, the Althing signed a treaty that made Norway's king the ruler of Iceland. The Althing hoped King Haakon would bring peace to the country.

Under Norwegian rule, the quality of life for Icelanders slowly **declined**. As the king's rights increased, the Icelandic people suffered. Promised imports to the island soon lessened. In 1380, Norway and Denmark united. Denmark then took control of Iceland.

After 1400, countries such as England and Germany sent people to Iceland to trade and fish the country's waters. The trading helped Iceland's **economy** for a time.

In the late Middle Ages, Iceland's economy declined. Many of the common birch trees were cut. And, there was too much grazing by farm animals. Together, this caused soil erosion and made it difficult to grow crops. At the same time, the climate became more severe.

Iceland in the 1500s

Life continued to be hard. From 1402 to 1404, the Black Death plague hit Iceland. One-third of the population died. In addition, the Danish monarchy stopped much of Iceland's fish trade by the mid-1500s. Around this same time, King Christian III of Denmark made Lutheranism Iceland's official religion. Many Icelanders were Catholic and resisted this change.

In 1602, Denmark began requiring merchants to purchase licenses in order to trade with Iceland. As a result, low-quality products sold for high prices. Many Icelanders became poor. And in 1662, Denmark's king officially took the last of the Althing's power.

Other disasters followed. From 1707 to 1709, Icelanders suffered an outbreak of a disease called smallpox. The population fell from about 50,000 to less than 40,000.

Between June 8, 1783, and February 1784, Mount Laki continuously erupted. It was the largest lava flow in recorded history. The volcanic gases killed crops and livestock, resulting in a severe scarcity of food. As a result, one-fifth of the population died.

Iceland began to see improvements in the 1800s. In 1843, a group of citizens successfully restored the Althing. And, Iceland was opened to trade with all nations in 1854. Iceland received a new **constitution** in 1874. It gave the Althing some legislative power and control over local funds.

Many Icelanders moved to North America in the 1880s. Meanwhile, Iceland's **economy** continued to improve. And the struggle for independence continued. In 1904, **home rule** was transferred to Iceland. On December 1, 1918, the Treaty of Union made Iceland a separate country under the Danish king.

In 1944, Icelanders voted to end the Treaty of Union. A new **republic** was created on June 17, 1944. Icelanders elected Sveinn Björnsson as their first president. The country joined the **United Nations** in 1946 and **NATO** in 1949. Throughout the rest of the century, Iceland worked to build up its fishing **fleet**.

In 1980, Icelanders elected Vigdís Finnbogadóttir as the country's first female president. In fact, Vigdís is the first woman in the world elected to chief of state!

Today, Iceland continues to have a small population. Almost 300,000 people call Iceland home. **Unemployment** is low, and the standard of living is high. The people continue to work to make Iceland a successful, prosperous nation.

Land of Natural Wonders

Iceland is a large island in the North Atlantic Ocean. It lies northwest of Scotland, west of Norway, and east of Greenland. The Greenland Sea borders Iceland to the north. The Denmark Strait is northwest. Iceland sits just south of the **Arctic Circle**.

Iceland is a **plateau** dotted with many mountains. The tallest point is Hvannadalshnúkur (HWAH-nah-dahlsh-noo-kur) at 6,952 feet (2,119 m).

Glaciers and cooled lava beds cover about 10 percent of the land. The largest glacier is Vatnajökull (VAHT-nah-yoo-koot-uhl). It covers more than 3,000 square miles (7,770 sq km). And, its thickest point is about 3,000 feet (900 m) deep!

Iceland sits on the Mid-Atlantic Ridge, a great underwater mountain chain. In addition, a **fault line** runs across the island. As a result, Iceland has many volcanoes and small earthquakes. Hekla is the best-known volcano.

The actual land is made up of cooled lava rock. Between 1963 and 1967, an underwater volcano erupted. This created the island of Surtsey, off the southwestern coast. Iceland's 200 volcanoes continue to shape the land.

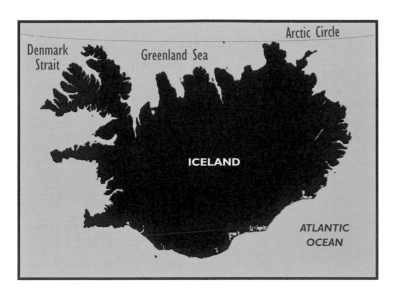

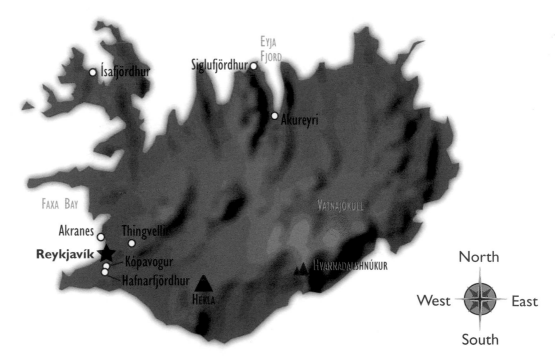

Iceland also has about 800 hot springs, geysers, and **solfataras**. The word "geyser" actually comes from a hot spring named Geysir located in the southern lowlands.

The barren central highlands are **uninhabited**. The western shore is cut by many **fjords** (fee-AWRDS) and harbors. This area provides good fishing but little land suitable for farming.

The east also has fjords and lowlands. The southern lowlands contain most of Iceland's farmable soil. The southeast is locked between glaciers and the ocean. The southwest features many lava fields and some natural harbors. This is where the country's best fishing grounds are located.

Iceland's weather is warmer than you might think. Reykjavík reaches about 52 degrees Fahrenheit (11°C) in July. In January, Reykjavík's average temperature is 31 degrees Fahrenheit (-1°C). The northwest has about 100 days of snow. But, it only snows about 40 days in the southeast. The **aurora borealis** can often be seen in autumn and early winter.

Iceland is a land of the midnight sun. In the summer, the sun shines continuously for about two to three months! But from mid-November to January, Iceland experiences only about four to five hours of sunlight each day.

Rainfall

AVERAGE YEARLY RAINFALL

Inches		Centimeters
Under 20		Under 50
20–40		50–100
40–60		100–150
Over 60		Over 150

Rain

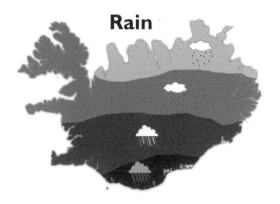

Temperature

AVERAGE TEMPERATURE

Fahrenheit		Celsius
Over 65°		Over 18°
54°–65°		12°–18°
32°–54°		0°–12°
21°–32°		-6°–0°
Below 21°		Below -6°

North

West ✦ East

South

Winter

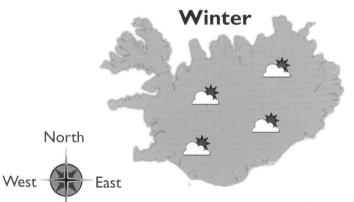

Summer

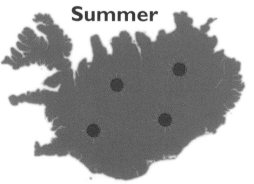

Nature

Only about one-fourth of Iceland's land has continuous vegetation. The moors and the **heaths** feature various low shrubs. These include heather, willow, dwarf birch, and berry plants. The lowlands contain many bogs and grasslands.

An early explorer gave Iceland its name. He was upset upon finding the coastal waters filled with ice. But, Iceland has a lot more to it than ice!

Few trees grow in Iceland. Birch trees were once numerous, but many forests were cut down. However, a government program that started in the 1950s has successfully replanted some of these forests.

Unique wildlife lives in Iceland. Seabirds such as fulmars, gannets, razorbills, and puffins nest on the sea cliffs. Golden plovers and whimbrels are often seen wading in the waters. And, there are at least 16 duck species. The eider duck is valued for its warm down feathers.

On land, birds of prey such as gyrfalcons, merlins, and some owls make their homes. Ravens, snow buntings, and ptarmigans (TAHR-mih-guhns) are also common. The white-tailed eagle was nearly extinct, but its numbers are increasing.

At the time of settlement, the arctic fox was Iceland's only native land mammal. However, reindeer were introduced and now **inhabit** the northeastern highlands. Mink were brought to the island and raised for their fur. They are now found in the wild. No reptiles or amphibians live in Iceland.

One of the world's largest puffin colonies is located in Iceland.

Seals and whales are often seen offshore. Silver-scaled herring, cod, and haddock are also common. Salmon, char, and trout are plentiful in the lakes and the rivers.

Icelanders

Icelanders are very proud of their language. They appreciate when visitors learn a phrase or two.

The people of Iceland are descended from Nordic and Celtic settlers. These early people spoke Old Norse. Modern Icelandic, the country's official language, is similar to this old language. All citizens speak Icelandic today. English, German, and other Nordic languages are spoken throughout Iceland, too.

Icelanders address each other by first name. This is because they don't have family names. Instead, a person's last name depends on his or her father's first name. For example, the son of a man named Erik would have the last name of Eriksson. The daughter of this same man would have the last name of Eriksdóttir. A woman does not change her name when she is married.

Iceland imports many goods, so prices are high. Even so, poverty is very low. Many women work outside the home because two incomes are necessary. The people have a high standard of living.

Most Icelanders live in urban areas. Modern homes built to withstand earthquakes are common. The country's numerous hot springs supply hot water to homes and cities.

Icelanders began building sod-covered homes because the forests were overcut. Thick blocks of turf covered a thin layer of wood. All of this was held together by a layer of living grass.

Education is important to Icelanders. So, almost all schools are free. All children are required to attend school until they are 16. Then, they may attend a four-year college. Following graduation, students may go to a university or a school specializing in teaching, art, nursing, or other studies.

Iceland enjoys freedom of religion. Most Icelanders belong to the Evangelical Lutheran Church. Some people attend Lutheran Free churches or Roman Catholic churches. Others have no specific religion.

Icelanders eat a lot of fish. Some distinctive Icelandic dishes are dried fish and carefully putrefied shark called

hákarl. Other dishes include gravlax, which is salmon marinated in salt and dill. *Hangikjöt*, or smoked lamb, is also popular. For dessert, many people enjoy cultured milk called *skyr* with sugar, cream, and bilberries.

For Icelanders, fish or lamb is a common main course at dinnertime.

Potatoes Browned in Sugar

Icelanders eat potatoes with most meals.

• 2 pounds white potatoes, peeled
• 1/8 pound butter
• 1/2 cup sugar

If possible, choose small potatoes. If the potatoes are large, cut them into equal pieces. Boil potatoes until tender. In a preheated saucepan, brown butter over low heat. Add sugar. When the mixture becomes frothy, add the potatoes. Repeatedly turn the potatoes until they are well coated and light brown in color.

AN IMPORTANT NOTE TO THE CHEF: Always have an adult help with the preparation and cooking of food. Never use kitchen utensils or appliances without adult permission and supervision.

LANGUAGE

English	Icelandic
Yes	Já (yow)
No	Nei (nay)
Please	Afsakið (AHF-sah-kihth)
Thank you	Takk fyrir (tak FIHR-ihr)
Good-bye	Bless (blehs)

Reel in the Profits

Iceland's **economy** has been determined by its location and climate. Fishing is the largest export industry, with about 830 ships in the country's **fleet**. In a good year, fishers may reel in nearly 1.8 million tons (1.6 million t)! They catch mostly capelins, herring, cod, and haddock.

Only a small part of the land is farmable. About 5 percent of Icelanders farm. Most farmers raise sheep for meat, wool, and skins. Dairy cows, poultry, and pigs are also important.

Hay and grass flourish in the long summer sun. It is also possible to grow potatoes, turnips, and other edible roots. Greenhouses allow farmers to raise flowers, vegetables, tomatoes, and even bananas.

About one-fourth of Icelanders work in industry, including manufacturing, mining, and power. Factories produce cement and fertilizer. Printing and publishing employ many people, too. In 1969, the opening of the Straumsvík aluminum **smelting** plant renewed the economy.

Fishing has long been important to the Icelandic people.

Iceland makes large use of geothermal energy and hydroelectricity. The earth's heat creates steam to power industrial machinery and warm greenhouses. And, hot springs heat many towns. A plant at Lake Mývatn uses geothermal energy to process the mineral diatomite. Hydroelectricity, or electricity created by waterpower, runs the Straumsvík aluminum plant.

Iceland trades for many of its goods. The people import grains, timber, machinery, transportation gear, and manufactured goods. In return, they export fish and fish products, farmed items, aluminum, and diatomite. Reykjavík is the largest port. It is also Iceland's transportation and commercial center.

Island Cities

In 2006, Iceland's population was only 299,388. About four-fifths of the country is **uninhabited**. Most people live in a narrow band along the seacoast and the **fjords** and in the southwestern valleys.

Reykjavík is Iceland's capital and largest city. It lies in southwestern Iceland on Faxa Bay. The city was founded in 874 and remained a small fishing village until the 1900s. Today, about three-fifths of all Icelanders live in the capital and surrounding areas.

Reykjavík is an **economic** and **cultural** center. This clean, modern city is home to the **parliament** building. Reykjavík's cultural sights include the University of Iceland, the National and University Library, and the Iceland Symphony Orchestra. The city also has many museums, such as the Reykjavík Art Museum and the Sigurjón Ólafsson Museum.

Iceland's second- and third-largest cities are Kópavogur and Hafnarfjördhur. However, they are both suburbs of Reykjavík. Iceland's next largest town is Akureyri (AH-koor-ay-ree).

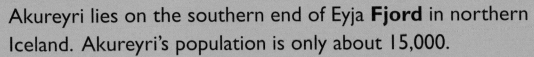

Akureyri lies on the southern end of Eyja **Fjord** in northern Iceland. Akureyri's population is only about 15,000.

Akureyri is an **economic** center. It is a fishing port and a manufacturing center for wool, fish, and other items. Shipbuilding, ironwork, and woodworking are important industries. Akureyri also has museums, botanical gardens, and a technical college.

Many Icelanders paint their houses pretty pastel colors.

From Here to There

Iceland was **isolated** from other countries until the late 1800s. About this time, steamships started visiting the island. Most roads in Iceland did not exist before the 1900s. The Icelandic pony served as the principal transportation mode.

Iceland has no railroads. So, people travel by bus, car, or airplane. And freight moves by truck. Major roads are paved. But many country roads are still gravel. The Hringvegur, or Ring Road, runs for about 900 miles (1,500 km) in a circle around the island.

Local air service takes people to various domestic airports. The international airport is located at Keflavík, near Reykjavík. Icelandair is the country's main airline. The **merchant marine** delivers most imports and exports by sea. They ship out of ports such as Reykjavík, Akranes, Ísafjördhur, and Siglufjördhur.

Telegraph cable, radio **satellite**, and the Internet link Iceland to the rest of the world. The first telegraph cable was connected to Iceland in 1906. Modern Icelanders commonly own televisions, radios, and telephones. About 225,000 people use the Internet.

Iceland has freedom of the press. However, political parties influence many Icelandic newspapers. Five daily and four weekly newspapers are published in Reykjavík. Many other weekly and biweekly newspapers and magazines are printed throughout the country.

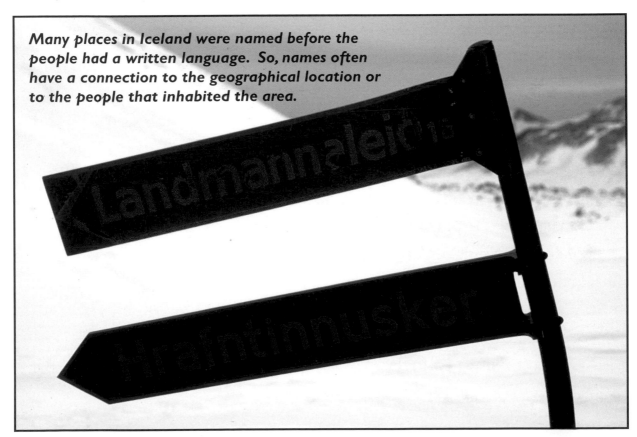

Many places in Iceland were named before the people had a written language. So, names often have a connection to the geographical location or to the people that inhabited the area.

World's First Parliament

Iceland is a **parliamentary democracy**. Its **constitution** was written in 1944 and guarantees people's civil rights. All citizens receive welfare benefits such as **pensions** and health insurance. Citizens who are at least 18 years old may vote for government leaders.

An elected president is head of state but has little power. He or she appoints the prime minister, cabinet members, and judges. The prime minister is the head of government. Together, the prime minister and the cabinet suggest and carry out government policies.

Iceland's settlers established the world's first **parliament**, the Althing, in 930. Today, most power lies with this one-house parliament. It passes the country's laws. The people elect 54 of the Althing's 63 seats. The political parties take the last nine seats. This balances the percentage of members each party has in the Althing. All 63 members serve for four years.

Iceland's lower judicial system divides into ordinary and special courts. District or town judges hear most cases brought before the ordinary courts. Others are sent to the special courts. The Supreme Court is the highest court. It hears appeals. Its nine judges serve for life. The country has no jury system.

For administrative purposes, the country is divided into 17 **provinces**. The provinces are further broken down into counties. Each area has a council that deals with local matters. The town councils choose the mayors.

Parliament building

Holidays and Festivals

Icelanders celebrate many holidays steeped in tradition. Some are religious, such as Maundy Thursday, Good Friday, and Easter. People also observe Ascension Day, Whitmonday, and Christmas.

Icelanders carry on **unique** traditions. On Bursting Day, Icelanders feast on salted meat and peas until they "burst"! On Ash Wednesday, people secretly pin small bags of ashes called *Öskupokar* to people's clothing. Children also run through the streets singing and collecting treats from the local shops.

Long ago, Icelanders considered winter and summer the only seasons. So, the people observe the first day of summer as a public holiday. They ring in summer with parades, sporting events, shows, and music.

Iceland became a **republic** in 1944. The people remember this on June 17, known as Iceland Republic Day. The greatest celebrations occur in Reykjavík. There, parades, street acts, and dancing are common activities. Throughout the country, people have picnics and participate in other organized festivities.

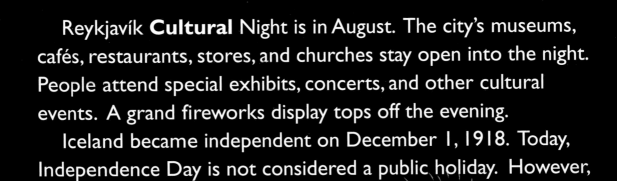

Reykjavík **Cultural** Night is in August. The city's museums, cafés, restaurants, stores, and churches stay open into the night. People attend special exhibits, concerts, and other cultural events. A grand fireworks display tops off the evening.

Iceland became independent on December 1, 1918. Today, Independence Day is not considered a public holiday. However, many people still celebrate.

Fireworks light up a chilly New Year's Eve in Reykjavík.